QUAILS
ABOUT RAISING QUAILS

Special Dedication

To every quail enthusiast

Acknowledgements

To every person who contributed towards making this a reality, I'm forever indebted to you. Thank you George, steve, Rachael, Brown And Amos for going out of your varied ways to bring this dream into fruition.

Contents

Page Number

Frequently Asked Questions

Did you know quails tend to lose their fertility as they age?

Below are the top most frequently asked questions and answers in regard to quail farming.

Question
Is it healthy to feed quail on chicken feeds?

Answer
First, it's important to note that quail are not poultry. They are game birds. Nonetheless, quail do comfortably feed on chicken feeds, but given that they are game birds, they need much higher protein content in their feeds as compared to chickens.

If you must give quail chicken feeds, ensure the feeds are supplemented with adequate relevant protein content. Significantly, quail chicks do need higher levels of protein in their diet (20-25%), to help them grow feathers and to put on good body weight.

If you therefore do the mistake of continuously feeding quail on un-supplemented chicken feeds (purely chicken feeds), they could temporarily exhibit outward signs of a normal growth, but inwardly severely starving from the right amounts of proteins they vitally need.

Question
Some of my birds have developed a tendency of leaving a huge dropping late in the evening or early in the morning. Should I be worried?

Answer

First, check if there could be any observable defects in the droppings like blood stains, or presence of any parasites such as worms or larvae. If there is none then you should have no cause for alarm. Such birds might have just taken too long before releasing the droppings. Equally, if it is a hen, then it could possibly be exhibiting broody-signs.

Question

How long should I store quail eggs before incubating them?

Answer

From my own experience, the hatching rate of the eggs is generally high at seven to eight days and below. Eggs older than seven days have a lower hatching rate. Significantly, eggs older than ten days tend to register minimal to sometimes nill hatching rate.

Question

What is the difference between Chinese painted quails and buttonquails (hemipodes)?

Answer

Buttonquails may physically appear to resemble quails, but are genetically unrelated to quails. The Chinese painted quails fall in the family of Phasianidae of order of Galliformes, while buttonquails (hemipodes) on the other hand are a small family of birds falling in the family of Turnicidae of the order of Charadriiformes.

Question
How can I tell a sick quail?

Answer
A sick quail may tend to exhibit some of the below general signs:

- **Numb, un-alert and unresponsive:** Sick quails may appear numb and un-alert. Many are generally unresponsive to any form of touch, and will mostly be seen bored or sleeping within their accommodation. If standing, they will tend to exhibit an abnormal posture.

- **Decline in egg production:** If there is a sudden drop in the number of eggs laid by the hens, that could a sign of disease infection within the flock.

- **Extreme body temperatures:** You should occasionally check the body temperatures of the birds to establish if any could be exhibiting unusually high or unusually low temperature as such could be a sign of sickness.

- **Lack of appetite:** Sick quails lack normal appetite and will resort to consuming reduced quantity of feeds.

- **Lackluster behavior:** Sick quails may appear gloomy, and are largely uninterested even when you give them feeds or water.

- **Observable defects in defecations**: When the defecation appears bloodstained, that could be a sure sign of internal infection. If it has an accompaniment of worms or larvae, that's a sign of possible parasitic infection. If it is hard, or watery, those could be signs of possible dehydration and diarrhea respectively.

- **Difficulty in breathing**: Blocked mucus membranes, or any observable or hearable sound suggesting difficulty in breathing by bird could be a sign of respiratory infection, possibly pneumonia.

- **Rough or loose plumage**: If the feathers are falling off, or appear rough in texture, be sure to check the bird closely for any possible disease or parasite infection.

Note: When you spot a bird exhibiting signs of sickness, isolate it from the rest of the flock, as fast as you possibly can. Afterwards, seek for the services of a trained and experienced poultry vet to help you diagnose and possibly treat the affected bird. Do not try to offer any form of treatment to a sick quail on your own if you aren't sure about the disease it might be suffering from. Things may turn tragic!!

Question
How long do quail eggs take to hatch?

Answer
The hatching period for incubated quail eggs varies from one quail breed to another. However, in general, the eggs take an

average of 16-18 days to hatch under proper incubation conditions. But there are certain domesticated breeds whose eggs may hatch as early as on the 14th or 15th day of incubation.

Question
How can I stimulate higher egg laying from the layers?

Answer
To stimulate higher production of eggs from the hens, you'll need to exercise the below:

- Raise a healthy flock free from disease infection.
- The hens should be young yet mature with known genetical ability to realize high production efficiency.
- Feed the hens on nutritious and well balanced feeds with plenty of clean and freshwater availed to them for drinking.
- Ensure correct amount of lighting for extended period of time (usually 14 hours each 24 hours).
- The hens must be raised under noise-free and disturbance free environment. Such distractions hinder their egg laying potential.

Question
How can I tell a fertile quail egg?

Answer
It can be a tough task for an average quail keeper to tell a fertile quail egg from an infertile one. However, there should be no cause for alarm. To start you off, you can use the below three observable signs to tell right away an infertile egg:

- Cracks on the eggshell.
- Absence of yolk or presence of double yolk. This can be detected via candling
- Dark spots/blood spots/ or bloody ring around or in the yolk. These too can be detected through candling.

The first step to guarantee fertility of a quail egg is through correct pairing of the birds, in the ratio of one male to a maximum of three females. Onwards, on the seventh day of incubation, you can candle the eggs. Using a candling lamp, a fertile egg will show a reddish embryo, while an infertile one will show a clear embryo.

But if unsure about the colors on the seventh day, you can again candle the eggs on the 13th or 14th day of incubation. If the chick is absent, you will see a larger section of the egg containing a clear embryo, with a tiny space containing air. But if the chick is present, the embryo will appear dark, or the light may not be able to penetrate through the eggshell.

Question
How can I yield a high hatch rate using artificial egg incubator?

Answer
To guarantee a high hatch rate using artificial egg incubator, you should exercise the below:
- Use fertile eggs seven days old and below.

- Before putting the eggs inside an incubator, ensure they are clean, fresh and free from abnormalities (you can candle them to ascertain this).

- Put the eggs at room temperature for a few hours before putting them inside the incubator.

- Ensure the incubator is properly cleaned and disinfected (properly sterilized).

- Remember, for an incubator to hatch any egg effectively, it has to provide three things namely: *suitable temperature, relative humidity, and satisfactory amount of fresh air to the incubated egg.*

- Turn the eggs, three times each 24 hours to ensure uniform heating, except during the last two days to hatching (day 15 and onwards).

Question
What should be the ideal amount of humidity inside an incubator?

Answer
During incubation, humidity should be constantly kept at around 40%-45%. But during the last 4 days to hatching, it should be upwardly adjusted to around 60%-65% to necessitate cracking of the egg shells.

Question
What should be the ideal temperatures inside an incubator?

Answer

37.5°c (99.5F) to 38°C (100.5F). However, since each incubator is uniquely designed, you should always read the manufacturer's manual on how best to handle handling the incubator.

Question
How best should I pair my quails to guarantee high yield?

Answer
If all you want is fertile eggs, simply pair one male to utmost three females (though pairing of one male to two females usually yield far much better results). Such right pairing not only yields high fertility rate but equally prevents the hens from fighting over the male, or from fighting the male.

If all you want is unfertilized eggs, you should never be worried about how best to pair the birds. You can even keep all males and females separate from one another. You can equally mix the males and females, but this will yield some fertilized eggs.

Notably, the right pairing of the birds is key when you are after fertilized eggs.

Question
What is the most ideal quail breed to raise?

Answer
The best type of quail bird to keep is largely dependent on your need or purpose for keeping quail. What's your main reason for keeping quail? World over, different people keep different breeds of quails for different reasons including, for provision of daily

fresh eggs, provision of meat, provision of both eggs and meat, as domestic pets, and for commercial gains.

Different quail breeds have different personalities. Before settling in on any breed, do enough research on your need for keeping the bird and the personality you would wish the breed to exhibit. Afterwards, visit a few established quail farmers or quail breeders within your locality to have that invaluable firsthand experience on raising the breed you are after. Summarily, the best type of quail breed to consider raising should meet your purpose of raising quail, and be both locally and readily available.

Summarized Basic Facts About Quail

Did you know a group of quails is called a covey, a bevy, or a flock?

As already noted, quail are not poultry! They are game birds in the family of Phasianidae. The Phasianidae is a large family of birds including jungle fowls, partridges, and old-world quails. (Dictionary.com describes old-world quails as *small game birds with a rounded body and small tail*).

In terms of physical appearance, quails are small and chubby in body size, and are covered in bluish to gray feathers. They are about 5.8 to 8.5 inches long, and weigh about 4 ounces.

There are several breeds of quail, in different strains and colors. In their natural habitat, they live as a flock and feed on grains, insects, plant leaves, and seeds.

Certain indigenous species of quails are migratory; they move as a flock from one place to another. Mostly, during winter, they flee to the northern parts of Africa, and in summer, they migrate to parts of Europe and Asia.

Across the globe, many people continue to domesticate quails largely for the birds' nutritious eggs and delicious meat.

A number of domesticated quail breeds can fly over a short distance. You should therefore raise them with lots of care.

Quails are susceptible to attack by predators such as cats, dogs, snakes, owls, skunks, eagles, foxes etc. While on their own in the wild, quail build their own nests on the ground using grass and other plant stems and leaves.

Certain breeds of male quail tend to make a distinctive sound (noise) for a short period of time; though they can make that sound over and over. They mostly make that sound out of excitement, in case they sense any looming danger, or feel lonely because of separation from female birds.

Four Vital Things To Help You Raise Healthy Quails

Did you know at one point in history, quail almost became extinct? Did you also know there are over 120 species of quails across the globe?

So you want to raise healthy quail? Below are the four vital essentials to help you realize that:

- **Go through lots of relevant and up-to-date information on quails and quail farming.**

  It's essential to know what you are getting into and how best you will effectively stay in it. It's that simple! Dig deep on quails and quail farming. Have enough relevant information on the latest developments in the quail farming industry, plus general market trends in the poultry farming segment. Afterwards, secure all the legal documents, if necessary, to guarantee noninterference from authorities or neighbors once you start keeping the birds.

  The more information you know on quails and quail farming, the more effective you will be at raising the birds.

- **Have the right breeds from the start, depending on your purpose for keeping the birds.**

  There is an old adage in the poultry world that if you start with a desirable breed, you should anticipate desirable output. But if you start with an undesirable breed, anticipate undesirable output. The quality of input is directly proportional to the quality of output. In summary, if you want to raise the birds for purposes of egg or meat production, get the right breeds with proven high yield potential. Don't try re-inventing the wheel.

- **Have a correct housing facility, or a secure space for safe rearing of quails**

  Whether you are raising the birds for domestic or commercial ends, on large scale or small scale, in cages or via free-range system, know quails thrive best where there is minimal distraction. Raise them in the right housing, with the right number of birds per unit – avoid overcrowding them. The housing should be located in a secure place with limited access to strangers, and no access to rodents. The location should be noise-free to encourage maximum yield.

- **Know about quail feeds and best disease management practices**

  To effectively raise healthy quail, you must arm yourself with the right knowledge on quail feeds and best disease management practices. This can never be overemphasized. In case you feel disadvantaged with such information or knowledge, it is advisable to readily seek for the services of trained and experienced quail professionals within your location.

Candling Quail Eggs

Did you know a quail's egg has up to four times the nutritional content found in a chicken's egg? And that a quail's meat is rich in Vitamin B Complex, Vitamin E and K, Iron, Phosphorus, Thiamine, Zinc, and Copper?

Egg candling is simply the act of examining an egg with an aim of detecting any defect or abnormality. Mostly, the egg is viewed against a source of light like a torch, sunlight, candle, or a specially designed candling lamp.

The most common egg abnormalities that can be detected through candling include:

- Cracks on the eggshell
- Absence of egg yolk, or presence of double yolk.
- Dark spots, blood spots or bloody ring around egg yolk or in the egg yolk.

Signs of good quail eggs suitable for incubation or even consumption

- Should be oval in shape.
- Should have a single yolk, centered and yellowish.
- Should be clean with a clear and firm eggshell.
- Should posses clear yet thick and firm albumen.
- Should be free of blood spots/meat spots around or in the yolk.

Signs of an abnormal quail egg

An egg abnormality may render it infertile and possibly unfit for human consumption. Summarily, below are some of the observable signs of an abnormal quail egg:

- **Soft eggshells or thin eggshells**

  Soft eggshells are usually a resultant of the hen prematurely laying the egg. It symbolizes lack of calcification in the egg which takes place in the shell gland. On the other hand, thin eggshells may symbolize disease infection or nutritional disorder.

- **Dark spots, blood spots or bloody ring around or in the egg yolk**

  The presence of blood clots or blood spots in an egg yolk is a sign of broken blood capillaries during ovulation. An egg with such characteristics may be possibly infertile, and even sometimes unfit for human consumption.

- **Abnormal color of the egg yolk**

  The color of a normal egg yolk is generally yellow. Any deviation from this may signify an abnormality.

- **Abnormal egg yolk**

  The absence of egg yolk or presence of double yolk in an egg would render it infertile and possibly unfit for human consumption.

How To Take Care Of Fertile Quails Eggs Before Incubation

Did you know you can comfortably cover quail eggs with a polythene plastic bag to help preserve their moisture before presenting them for incubation?

How you handle fertile quail eggs once laid by hens is central to determining the hatching rate to anticipate from such eggs. Truth is, it's one thing to get a high percentage of fertile eggs from the hens, and it's another thing to realize a high hatching rate from the same eggs.

You must therefore exercise a certain degree of care when handling fertile quail eggs.

As already noted, in order to guarantee high fertility rate of the laid eggs, you should have the males and females paired in the right ratio. One male to utmost three females may be considered ideal, but one male to two females is most effective, yielding better results (usually over 80% fertility rate).

Collect the laid eggs daily, two to three times each day. This is necessary to prevent them from getting dirty and from losing their shell moisture content. Timely collection of the eggs is equally essential towards baring the birds from trying to crack the eggs.

Whenever picking or moving the eggs from one point to another, handle them with utmost care as they have a delicate outer shell layer.

Once collected, store the eggs at room temperature, in a humid location as they await incubation. Alternatively, temperatures of around 50^0F and an average humidity of 65% are considered ideal.

Ensure the eggs are incubated at seven days and below. Eggs older than ten days have low to nil hatch rates.

Before setting the eggs inside an incubator, ensure they are clean and that the incubator is rightly sterilized.

Quail Egg Incubation

Did you know you can successfully incubate quail eggs inside any normal chicken-type egg incubator?

Since most domesticated quails seldom go broody, the ideal way to hatch their eggs is through use of an artificial egg incubator.

Interestingly, quail eggs can be comfortably hatched by use of a number of commercially available egg incubators, though you must fittingly set the eggs in suitable trays, and adjust the incubator to right conditions favorable to hatching the eggs.

When using any commercial egg incubator, ensure you effectively go through the manufacturer's manual or usage recommendations from the manufacturer in order to yield favorable results.

The incubator must first be cleaned and correctly disinfected. Thereafter, test its ability to provide the right temperatures, correct humidity, and proper ventilation to the incubated eggs.

As already noted, before setting the eggs inside the incubator, ensure they are fertile, clean and less than ten days old.

Once the eggs are correctly set in the incubator, you should religiously turn them at 180^0, except during the last two to three days to hatching. Significantly, avoid turning the eggs during the last 48 hours to hatching. Doing so might negatively affect the already forming chicks.

In case you are using an electric enabled artificial egg incubator, but you reside in a location prone to power blackouts, have a standby power back up, or an alternative source of power like a generator. The power back up will help you maintain the right incubator's temperature. Any prolonged unfavorable temperature conditions inside the incubator can make the incubated eggs be susceptible to going stale instead of hatching.

Reasons For Poor Egg Hatch And Possible Solutions For Each Case

Did you know in the twentieth century, Egypt was the leading exporter of quails; exporting over three million quails annually?

Below are the top five reasons for poor egg hatch, and possible solutions for each case.

Incubating infertile eggs

It can be a painful ordeal to stay optimistic in wait for chicks to hatch from incubated infertile eggs! In fact it would be miraculous should the infertile eggs hatch!

Solution

To help curb this, you should candle the eggs before presenting them for incubation. Again, once incubated, candle them – but before the 15th day of incubation to help detect infertile eggs. But going through the egg candling procedure, correctly pair the males and the females to guarantee high chances of fertility of the laid eggs.

Incubating abnormal eggs

As well outlined under egg candling, an egg may be classified as abnormal (an egg with a defect), if it has cracks on its outer shell, its shell is contaminated, has presence of double egg yolk, or absence of the yolk, or has very dark spots or blood ring around, or in its yolk. The chances of hatching fertile abnormal eggs are usually lower.

Solution

Again, before presenting the eggs for incubation, candle them to ensure that abnormal eggs or eggs with defects do not see the inside of an incubator. It's that simple!

Failure to turn the eggs/irregular turning of the eggs inside the incubator

The main reason for turning the eggs during incubation is to guarantee uniform heating of the incubated eggs. Failure to do so or irregular turning of the eggs may result into overheating of one side of the eggs, thus making them unreliable for hatching chicks.

Solution

During incubation, religiously, commit to turn the eggs, at least three times every twenty four hours. Equally, you can use an automatic egg incubator with a proven ability to urn the eggs at 180^0, at least three times each 24 hours.

Lack of favorable conditions inside the incubator

Remember, for a fertile egg to be hatched, the incubator has to provide: suitable temperature, relative humidity, and adequate amount of fresh air to the incubated egg. If the incubator you are using can't provide these three then be rest assured the incubated eggs will most probably fail to hatch.

Solution

As you incubate the eggs, always use incubators with proven potential to hatch eggs. Equally, if you reside in an area which experiences several power failures, you should have a power back up to stabilize the incubator during power blackouts.

The eggs may appear fertile when candled, but still fail to hatch chicks when incubated in the right incubator

Sometimes you may incubate fertile eggs using properly functioning incubator but still fail to realize hatching of the eggs.

Fertile eggs may fail to hatch due to a number of reasons such as incubating eggs from older breeds of quails or incubating eggs which have taken too long after being laid.

Solution

Always incubate eggs from younger but mature breeds of quails. Equally, incubate eggs which are utmost 7-8 days old and below. And most important, ensure the incubator is clean, disinfected and functioning well.

How To Raise Quail Chicks In The Right Way

Did you know one of the leading causes of deaths in quail chicks is through drowning in waterers?

The process of taking care of young quail chicks is known brooding.

Once the fertile eggs have successfully hatched into chicks, you should remove the chicks from the incubator and transfer them to a brooder; a specially built structure where food, water and other relevant essentials necessary for the growth of the chicks are provided.

Below are the necessities inside a good brooder.

A good source of heat

A good source of heat is necessary to help heat up and regulate the temperature inside the brooder. Sources of heat may be in form of electric bulbs, gas burners, charcoal burners etc.

The brooder should be correctly heated all the time. The two best ways to verify this is by use of a thermometer, and or by closely watching behavior/movements/positions of the chicks around the heating source. If the chicks are crowding around the heating source, that's a sign for presence of cold in the incubator. But if they are hiding at the walls of the incubator (away from the heating source), that's a sign for too much heat in the brooder.

The temperature inside the brooder should be kept at 95F during the first week, and should thereafter be lowered by at least 5F on each passing week until the 4th week when the birds are ready to be taken out of the brooder.

When the brooder is correctly heated, the chicks should be evenly spread and will be seen normally going about their business. Gradually, withdraw the source of heat by the fourth week to allow the birds to adapt to the surrounding environment.

Litter

The main work of a litter inside a brooder is to help in keeping the brooder warm by absorbing wet moisture. The litter may be in form of sawdust, wood shavings, or paper cuttings. And since most quail chicks may have difficulty differentiating saw dust from their feeds, I prefer use of paper cuttings as bedding of the brooder. Already used litter should be timely discarded from the brooder to curb spread of contagious diseases like pneumonia and bad odor.

Waterers

The waterers should be set up in such a way that the chicks cannot step or defecate on them. The drinking water should be available in adequate portion, clean, fresh, and placed at convenient locations to avoid stressing the birds.

Fill the waterers with glass marbles or pebbles to bar the chicks from drowning in them. One of the leading causes of early mortality in quail chicks is by drowning in the waterers.

Don't forget to have the waterers cleaned thoroughly before filling up (you should clean them daily). And after two weeks, you can remove the glass marbles /pebbles from the drinking water.

Feeders

Clean and adequate feeders should be placed at convenient locations where chicks do not strain to access them. The feeders too, should be made in such a way that the chicks do not step or defecate on them.

Well-balanced feeds rich in protein should be readily available and given to the chicks at all times. As a good recommendation, you can feed them on game bird feeds /turkey feeds (a starter with an average protein component of 25%.

Once the birds are four weeks old, you should prepare to change their feeds to layers mash. By this time, you should have moved them to the cages. Most domesticated breeds of quail do start laying eggs at 6 weeks. Therefore, you should effectively change their feeds to layers mash as they approach the egg laying stage.

Enough ventilation

There should be adequate circulation of fresh air in the brooder. This is to allow for gaseous exchange and to keep contagious respiratory infections at bay.

Correct amount of light

The brooder should be correctly lit to allow the chicks to see the feeds and water. For small-scale, a heating bulb can as well serve the purpose of lighting the brooder and that of providing necessary heat.

Note: The brooder should be located at an ideal location away from noise and disturbance, and should securely built to protect the chicks from predators. Equally, always exercise good grooming when handling the chicks, and ensure that they are raised under sanitary conditions.

Depending on their physical appearance, on the 3rd or 4th week, you should transfer the birds from the brooder to the cages, or to an appropriate housing.

If you want to raise cannibal-free birds, you should debeak the birds at two to three weeks of age. One improvised way of exercising debeaking is through use of a nail clipper.

Housing – The Three Most Common Options

Did you know a number of quail breeds are good aviary cleaners?

Below are the three most common housing options for keeping quails.

- **Use of cages.**
- **Use of a coop/pen or house.**
- **Use of an aviary.**

Use of Cages

Most of quail cages are specially built using wood and wire mesh. If you plan to house the birds in cages, a good recommendation is to use 2 sq ft per bird.

Construct the floor of the cages with wire mesh capable of easily letting the birds' droppings to fall off the cages. The mesh should equally be capable of barring predators from attacking quail.

There are two ways of acquiring the cages. First, you can buy already built cages from local dealers/breeders/suppliers, or secondly, you can build your own. When raising quails inside a cage, ensure the cages are roomy enough to avoid stressing the birds. Stressed birds are usually unproductive.

Use of a Coop/Pen or House

Here, quail are kept in a typical house-like structures, and are provided with necessities such as feeds, drinking water, a source of heat (for the chicks), and protection from predators.

Most people prefer to have quail pens or coops placed outdoors due to an ammonium-like smell contained in the birds' droppings.

If raised on the floor or solid ground, consider spreading wood shavings or sawdust. This makes cleaning of the birds' droppings from the coop to be easy. (With a spread of wood shavings on the floor, the droppings will be absorbed by the shavings to form dry crumbs which are easy to clean out of the accommodation).

In case you have any unutilized building in the farm, say like some shed or even a barn, you can turn it into a coop by covering it properly with recommended wire mesh. Doing so will help protect the birds from predators. The birds will equally lack any space to escape from the house.

Use of an aviary

An aviary is an enclosure with adequate space for the housed birds to move around freely. Interestingly, since quail have a cool personality, keeping them inside the aviary may result into lower egg production; especially if other birds are equally housed in the same aviary.

Also, due to the exposed nature of most aviaries, quail may be negatively affected by extreme temperatures; too hot or too cold temperatures may have adverse effects on their health.

On the other hand, a quail breed like the Chinese painted quail is a known aviary cleaner. It can comfortably feed on the feeds spilled on the floor of the aviary by other others. It will therefore help keep the aviary clean by feeding on food wastes, and in return, help you save on feed costs..

Note

In case you want to let quail to roam freely in any open field, clip their wings to prevent them from hopping away. Quails have a tendency to fly short distances and thus, can easily vanish if let in the open. In fact, many quail keepers have lost the birds due to releasing them in the open without properly clipping their wings.

Feeding Quail

Did you know in the wild, quail feed on berries, seeds, insects, nuts, roots and leaves of certain plants and trees? And that millet isn't nutritionally complete to be regarded as a full meal to quail birds?

It is recommended domesticated quail be fed on non-medicated game bird feed since it has high protein content.

The feeders should be thoroughly cleaned before each fill. Afterwards, simply half-fill them to prevent cases of feed spillage.

Adequate, clean and disinfected waterers should equally be availed and placed at convenient locations for the birds to drink from. The waterers should be filled with clean and freshwater at room temperature. Do not give them hot or cold water as they will shy away from drinking such.

An egg is composed of over 50% water. Therefore, the absence of drinking water would positively translate into inability of the birds to lay eggs. It's that simple!

Occasionally, treat the birds with meal worms and other insects such as crickets, grasshoppers, and wax worms. Similarly, hang vegetables or greens within the cages (the vegetables or greens should be free from sprays of pesticides). Also, you can feed the birds on fruits like apples cut into small pieces.

Give the birds sand as grit to aid in food digestion.

When the hens begin laying eggs, give them oyster shells or limestone to boost them with calcium which is invaluably essential to help in the calcification of the eggs. Lack of calcium may result in the formation and subsequent laying of eggs with weak shells.

When you keep healthy quails and feed them effectively on the right diet with correct amounts of nutrients, plus clean and freshwater for drinking made available to them, they will reward you with laying some of the most nutritious eggs you have ever tasted. You will equally be guaranteed of a delicious meat at your disposal.

Sexing - How To Tell If Quail Is Male Or Female

Did you know Japanese quail can mate for life? However, over the years, several mutants of Japanese quail have emerged that have no regard to mating for life.

How can you tell a male quail from a female one? Unless you have prior experience in handling quail, this might seem like some tricky puzzle to solve.

Given that there are various different types (breeds) of quails out there, being able to tell whether one is male or female can turn out to be a daunting task. However, it isn't supposed to be like that! There are various ways to use in distinguishing a male quail from a female one, and below are the four topmost ways:

By checking on the physical appearance

A number of female quails appear bigger in physical appearance when compared with their male counterparts of same breed and age. Summarily, the females will tend to appear slightly bigger than the males of the same breed and age.

By observing the color patterns on the birds' chests

Going this route is largely ideal for quails with speckled feathers like the Japanese quail. The female quails have speckled feathers on their chests while the male ones have plain feathered chests.

Examining quail's vent or cloaca

This is one of the most effective ways of distinguishing a male quail from a female one. There are two ways of examining the vent. First, when you press the area around it with your two fingers, a small ball-like lump may pop forward suggesting the bird is male. If the ball-like lump fails to show up then the bird is female.

Secondly, when you press the vent, you may see presence of some white foam coming out of it, suggesting the bird is male. You would not see the foam in females.

Roosting of the male birds

At five weeks, many breeds of male quails begin to roost (they begin to make some sound or noise). If you can patiently wait for the five weeks then you will have the perfect opportunity to be able to tell the male quails from the females from that roosting.

How To Raise Healthy Quails

Did you know through exercising good sanitation and feeding quail on well-balanced feeds, you can add two to three years to their lifespan?

Quail is regarded to be in a state of good health when all of its body organs and systems are normal and functioning well.

Below are the gains of keeping healthy quail.

- Production of high quality eggs and meat. I believe you may not like to see your quails lay eggs which have, say, attachments of any parasitic larvae. You want them to lay clean and fresh eggs.
- Healthy quails have inability to spread any contagious diseases among themselves, and to humans too.
- Healthy quails are vibrant, mature fast and have a longer lifespan. They are generally associated with high productivity.
- Healthy quails are cost-effective to raise. You will have minimal or no bills related to their treatments.
- Unlike sick quail, healthy quail have a higher market value. They fetch higher prices.

Just like human beings, quails too need relevant and adequate care to grow and remain healthy. Below are some of the practices you can adopt to help you raise healthy quails.

- Occasionally, expose the birds to sunlight. They need that precious sunlight's vitamin D to help them develop strong bones. Exposure to sunlight also excites them and thus improves their productivity.

- Give them nutritious and well-balanced feeds in adequate quantities.
- Give the birds clean and freshwater for drinking, at room temperature. Avoid giving them hot or very cold water.
- Provide them with grit to aid in food digestion.
- Hang some greens (vegetables) within their accommodation to supplement their feeds. The greens too will help keep them busy as they continually peck on them.
- Always exercise good grooming and sanitation. Handle the birds gently during culling or when being vaccinated, and raise them under a clean environment. This can never be overstated!
- To help contain spread of diseases, it is advisable to disinfect the birds, the cages, the waterers, and the feeders correctly with recommended disinfectors. External parasites such as ticks, lice, and mice may attack the birds under unsanitary conditions and infect them with life threatening diseases such as histomoniasis (histomonosis).
- Raise the birds in a peaceful environment. Like most breeds of poultry, quails too detest noisy surroundings. They will register a decline in productivity when raised in a noisy environment.

In a nutshell, when your quails are well fed, happy and disease free, you will be guaranteed a higher productivity, all the time.

Japanese Quail (*Coturnix Japonica*)

Did you know the Japanese name for quail bird is uzura?

It is important to cover Japanese quail in some summarized detail since it's one of the most common quail breed raised for either commercial or domestic production of eggs or meat, or both.

The Japanese quail, also known as Coturnix japonica, is a species of the old-world quail. The old-world quail is a group including *the Brown quail, the New Zealand quail, Canary Islands quail, the Blue quail, the King quail and the Common quail.*

The Japanese quail is native to Asia, Europe, and Africa. Interestingly, today's domesticated Japanese quail is an inter-breed of the species from these locations. It has an identical physical likeness to the Common quail (*Coturnix coturnix*); which is purely terrestrial and lives in the wild.

In their native locations, Japanese quails are migratory birds and averagely grow to between 18-23cm in height. An adult Japanese quail may consume 15 to 19 grams of food every day. Fascinatingly, some breeds of the Japanese quail mate for life!

If you are in search of a quail breed which is commercially suitable for egg or meat production, Japanese quail is a good bet. For production of daily fresh eggs at your backyard or meat (for domestic consumption), the Japanese quails will too, help you achieve that.

They are good table birds since they mature fast and are favorably resistant to a number of poultry diseases.

Did you know Japanese quail have the ability to incubate their eggs successfully? However, over the years, several mutants of the bird with no ability to go broody have continued to be developed. Improved plumage color, improved color of eggshells, and improved shape of their bodies have all been part of the motivating reasons behind the developments of these new mutants.

Chinese Painted Quail (*Coturnix chinensis*)

Did you know in the Bible, God fed the Israelites with quail? Exodus 16:13, and Numbers 11:31 notes that when the Israelites were fleeing from Egypt to the promised land of Canaan, God, on two occasions, provided them with plenty of quails as food.

Again, another interesting quail breed to cover in summarized detail is the Chinese painted quail due to its preference in being raised as an ornamental bird in most aviaries.

The Chinese painted quail has various names. It is referred to as the King quail, the Asian blue quail, and the blue-breasted quail. Notably, a number of Americans refer to the Chinese painted quail as Button quail since their chicks are *the size of a button.*

Chinese painted quail should not be confused with button quail (Turnix); the two are genetically unrelated. Chinese painted quail fall in the family of *Phasianidae* of the order of *Galliformes,* while button quail (Turnix), also known as hemipodes, are a small family of birds falling in the family of *Turnicidae* of the order of *Charadriiformes.* Button quail (Turnix) are not quail at all! They are more related to cranes and rails than to quails.

One distinctive characteristic of Chinese painted quail is the presence of a larger breast-bone, larger than those found in other quail birds. Significantly, that larger breast-bone has many muscles surrounding it, making it ideal as a table bird. And in terms of physical appearance, the Chinese painted quails are much smaller than other quail species such as the Japanese quails. In fact, they are regarded as the "smallest true quails".

They have a lifespan of between 3-5 years. Interestingly, the male Chinese painted quail appear more colorful than the female one. The male has a blue and brown flecked crown and back. Its breast and tail plumage are reddish brown in color, while its chin downwards is littered with a distinctive black and white stripping. On the other hand, the female has a slightly darker back than its abdomen with what looks like a white patch on its throat. It has an overall speckled brownish color from its fine black and white specks. However, both sexes have brown eyes with black beaks. Male Chinese painted quails emit a low growl sound.

Notably, Chinese painted quail is the most widely kept ornamental quail breed in most aviaries because of its prettiest and most colorful physical appearance. They are good aviary cleaners as they can comfortably feed on the feeds spilled by other birds. However, you should not keep them with other aggressive birds which might prey on them as food, or for fun.

It's advisable using one pair per aviary flight.

You should let them out of their accommodation with lots of precaution as they have the ability to fly over a five-foot wall or fence. If frightened, they exhibit quick bursts in an attempt to run for cover. They flap their wings hard and can easily break their necks when landing.

Chinese painted quail can too be kept in proper cages and in a well built coop as table birds and for egg production. They can breed all year round and lay over 200 eggs per year with good care. Equally, they help in spider catching in a growing number of butterfly breeding houses.

There are various mutants of the Chinese Painted quail. They exist in dominant colors of golden pearl, blue face and normal with recessive colors of silver and white. Equally, other mutations also exist in red breasted, red breasted silver, fawn, cinnamon, ivory, and ivory pearl colors.

Note

When the chicks of Chinese painted quail are ready to hatch, they signal each other and coordinate their hatching to ensure they all come out of the eggshells at once. And just after two weeks, these chicks are able to begin jumping up and down. If raised in the cages, you need to use extra small gauge wire mesh as a bedcover since the chicks are usually tinny and can go through the holes of most wire mesh.

Other Books By The Author

Selling Is Not For Cowards: 12 Sales Principles To Help You Sell Stronger, Smarter, And More Successfully

Quail Farming For Beginners: Everything You Need To Know

Millionaire Chicken Farmer: With Just One Rooster, Three Hens, And $50, She Became The Wealthiest Chicken Farmer In Detroit.

Profitable Chicken Rearing: Raising Chickens For Meat And Eggs, & Markets And Marketing Strategies.

Finding Yourself: How To Tap Into Your Potential And Live The Life You Were Created For

Brazil: Insights

Backyard Chickens For Beginners: Everything You Need To Know

The 4 Painful Life Stories: How We Contracted Hiv/Aids

THE END

28320427R00047

Printed in Great Britain
by Amazon